The Selfish Giant

A children's musical
Based on the short story by Oscar Wilde

Music, lyrics and adaptation
by David Perkins

Additional lyrics by Caroline Dooley

Samuel French — London
New York - Toronto - Hollywood

© 2003 BY DAVID PERKINS AND CAROLINE DOOLEY

This play is fully protected under the Copyright Laws of the British Commonwealth of Nations, the United States of America and all countries of the Berne and Universal Copyright Conventions.

All rights including Stage, Motion Picture, Radio, Television, Public Reading, and Translation into Foreign Languages, are strictly reserved.

No part of this publication may lawfully be reproduced in ANY form or by any means — photocopying, typescript, recording (including video-recording), manuscript, electronic, mechanical, or otherwise—or be transmitted or stored in a retrieval system, without prior permission.

SAMUEL FRENCH LTD, 52 FITZROY STREET, LONDON W1T 5JR, or their authorized agents, issue licences to amateurs to give performances of this play on payment of a fee. **This fee is subject to contract and subject to variation at the sole discretion of Samuel French Ltd.**

Licences for amateur performances are issued subject to the understanding that it shall be made clear in all advertising matter that the audience will witness an amateur performance; that the names of the authors of the plays shall be included on all programmes; and that the integrity of the authors' work will be preserved.

The publication of this play does not imply that it is necessarily available for performance by amateurs or professionals, either in the British Isles or Overseas. Amateurs and professionals considering a production are strongly advised in their own interests to apply to the appropriate agents for consent before starting rehearsals or booking a theatre or hall.

ISBN 0 573 08123 9

THE SELFISH GIANT

First performed at the Yvonne Arnaud Theatre, Guildford on 12th July 1995 by the Yvonne Arnaud Youth Theatre ACT 2 with the following cast:

Gardeners	Vicki Jesman
	Anna Jones
	Sian Jones
	Kevin Matthews
	Hannah Stone
Flowers	Katy Barwell
	Polly Everson
	Sarah Slater
Birds	Ruth Bremner
	Amanda Duffield
Children	Lucy Barwell
	Rosie Dalling
	Andrew Dickinson
	Emma Dickinson
	Natalia Goldman
	Nikki Lockwood
	Emma Martin
	Gemma Matthews
	Jonathan Slater
	Zoe Thompson
	Abigail Thorncroft
	Katy Thorncroft
	Jo Whiteman
Giant	Tom Gildon
Cornish Ogre	Victoria Brown
Snow	Neil Dennis
Frost	Kit Stokes
North Wind	Alex Stevenson
Hail	Laura Kirker
The Child	Rebecca Dale

Directed by Julia Burgess
Musical direction by David Perkins
Lighting design by Matthew Eagland and John Harris
Sound design by James Leatherby

CHARACTERS

Gardener 1
Gardener 2
Gardener 3
Gardener 4
Flowers
Birds
Children
Giant
Cornish Ogre
Snow
Frost
North Wind
Hail
The Child

MUSICAL NUMBERS

Overture

Section 1	**The Garden**	Gardeners, Flowers, Birds
Section 2	**How Happy We Are**	Children
Section 3	**The Giant's Return**	Gardeners, Giant, Cornish Ogre, Children
	Section 4a Build a Wall (Long Version)	Giant, Gardeners
	Section 4b Build a Wall (Short Version)	Giant, Gardeners
Section 5	**Outside the Garden**	Gardeners, Children - with solos
Section 6	**Inside the Garden**	Gardeners, Giant, Flower
Section 7	**Winter**	Gardeners, Snow, Frost, Wind, Hail
Section 8	**The Giant Laments**	Giant, Gardeners, Snow, Frost, Wind, Hail
Section 9	**Awakenings**	Gardeners, Giant, Children, Flowers, Birds, Snow, Frost, Wind, Hail
Section 10	**The Corner of the Garden**	Gardeners, Giant, The Child, Children
Section 11	**Harmony**	Children, Gardeners, Giant
Section 12	**The Passage of Time**	Gardeners, Giant, Children
Section 13	**The End?**	Gardeners, Snow, Frost, Wind, Hail, Giant, The Child, Children

Section 14 Anthem — Ensemble

   14a Bows

   14b Encore — Ensemble

   14c Exit Music (1)

   14d Exit Music (2)

Please see Music Notes regarding hire of band parts or backing CD on page x

IMPORTANT INFORMATION

Alterations to the script and score

If changes, additions or cuts to the show are required to make it work for a particular group, any proposed alterations (no matter how small) MUST be approved by the authors before rehearsals commence. Approval can be sought via Samuel French Ltd or directly from the authors via email: dperkins@dp-music.co.uk

The authors are happy to provide suggestions for such things as cuts, scene change music, chorus character names and so on. Making contact with them is easy, and they will consider any request. Making small changes this way is free of charge and it turns an illegal alteration into a legal one.

Cover illustration

Please note that the cover illustration remains the copyright of the artist, Simon Pearsall. Permission MUST be obtained prior to use of this illustration for publicity purposes, programmes, website graphics, or for any other purpose. Please contact Samuel French Ltd for details.

Use of music in schools and colleges for educational purposes

In purchasing this book we automatically convey the right to use all of the material in the classroom for teaching and instruction purposes, for assembly or collective worship.

Video and Audio recordings

In certain circumstances, permission may be given for a video or audio recording of your show to be made. Please apply to Samuel French Ltd for full details. Video and audio recordings made without prior permission are STRICTLY not allowed, even for archival or training purposes.

SYNOPSIS

Section 1 The Garden: The Gardeners are working in a garden. They describe it as full of beautiful flowers, trees and birds. They tell us that it belongs to the Giant who is currently away in Cornwall visiting his friend the Cornish Ogre.

Section 2 How Happy We Are: The Children of the village creep into the garden and play.

Section 3 The Giant's Return: Meanwhile the Giant is preparing to leave Cornwall and bids farewell to his friend. He returns to find his garden full of children. He throws them out.

Section 4 Build a Wall: The Giant explains how he intends to build a high wall around his garden to keep everybody out. The Gardeners tell us how the Romans during the reign of the Emperor Hadrian and the Ancient Chinese built walls to keep the peace. The Giant builds the wall with the help of the Gardeners and puts up a threatening sign – "TRESPASSERS WILL BE EATEN!"

Section 5 Outside the Garden: Outside the garden, the Children walk about miserably and talk of happier times when they used to play in the Giant's beautiful garden.

Section 6 Inside the Garden: The Gardeners explain that although spring has arrived, it is always winter in the Giant's garden. Nature's way of punishing him for his selfishness.

Section 7 Winter: The Giant looks out at the wintry scene. Snow, Frost, North Wind and Hail come to visit his garden.

Section 8 The Giant Laments: Inside his castle, the Giant cannot understand why spring has not yet come. He complains about the weather, how cold and miserable he is and how his water pipes have frozen. Outside in the garden the Snow, Frost, Wind and Hail make a terrible nuisance of themselves.

Section 9 Awakenings: One morning the Giant hears music coming from the garden. Looking out, he sees that the birds have returned and the garden is bursting with spring. The Children creep in through a hole in the wall and, convinced that the Giant must be dead, start playing once again. The Giant watches with delight.

Section 10 The Corner of the Garden: The Giant notices one small child in the corner of the garden where strangely it is still winter. The little boy, who seems a lot weaker than the other children, is unable to join in with their games and cannot climb the tree. The Giant's heart melts and at long last he realizes how selfish he has been. Determined to help the frail child he walks into the garden. The Children flee in terror except for the one child who is crying and does not see the Giant coming. The Giant walks up to the child and lifts him gently into the tree. The other children who have been watching realize that the Giant must have changed and return to the garden to befriend him. To prove that he is now a friendly and unselfish person, the Giant knocks down the wall and makes the garden free for all.

Section 11 Harmony: The Giant asks the Children who the little child was and where he had come from — he has since disappeared. The Children don't know him and they have never seen him before.

Section 12 The Passage of Time: Years pass and generations of children come and play with the Giant. He is now an old man, but cannot forget the little child that broke his heart all those years before.

Section 13 The End?: One morning, winter returns to the garden. The Giant does not mind — he knows that spring will return again in time. In one corner, however, he notices that it is still spring and sees the little child that he had helped long ago. Excitedly, he rushes over to the child and discovers that there are strange wounds on the Child's hands and feet. The Child tells the Giant that they are the "Wounds of Love". He says that because the Giant had once let him play in the garden he must now come and play in *his* garden "which is paradise". The Child leads the Giant away.

Section 14 Anthen: The children return to discover that the Giant has gone. The garden will be theirs for all time

PRODUCTION NOTES

CHARACTER BREAKDOWN / COSTUME SUGGESTIONS

Gardeners
There are four Gardeners who act as narrators. They communicate directly with the audience and are always slightly removed from the main action. They need to be confident singers both individually and as a group.
COSTUME SUGGESTIONS: Overalls/dungarees, wellies, etc.
SECTIONS: One or more Gardeners speak or sing a line in every section of the show.

Flowers
These are a small group of younger children who can be used throughout the show as much or as little as seems appropriate. They can join in with the Chorus singing if required, help the Gardeners to change scenery and generally act as colourful set dressing. They should be able to move well. One of the flowers has to perform a short dance and speak a few lines of dialogue.
COSTUME SUGGESTIONS: Yellow flower petal head-dresses; yellow dresses.
SECTIONS: The Garden, Inside the Garden (solo dance and dialogue), Awakenings, other songs (optional) as per Chorus.

Birds Like the Flowers, they can join in whenever it is felt to be appropriate.
COSTUME SUGGESTIONS: Yellow dresses; green beaks.
SECTIONS: The Garden, Awakenings, other songs (optional) as per Chorus.

Children of the Village (Chorus)
These are a group of Children of any age that act as the Chorus. There is a lot of singing, dancing and moving, with a chance for several of them to sing a solo.
COSTUME SUGGESTIONS: School uniform — contemporary or from a specific era, for example, the 1940s.
SECTIONS: How Happy We Are, The Giant's Return, Outside the Garden (with solos), Awakenings, The Corner of the Garden, Harmony, The Passage of Time, The End?, Anthem (with solos), Encore.

Giant
Strong acting and singing ability is required for this part. The Giant should be easily distinguishable from the rest of the company. You could use either a teacher or an older student to play the role or alternatively, create the Giant using a puppet with his voice sung off stage
COSTUME SUGGESTIONS: A beard, heavy boots, clothes fit for a Giant!
SECTIONS: The Giant's Return, Build a Wall, Inside the Garden, The Giant Laments, Awakenings, The Corner of the Garden, Harmony, The Passage of Time, The End?, Encore.

Cornish Ogre
This character only has one line and appears in one very short scene. One of the chorus could play him/her. It could be quite amusing to use the smallest child to play this part.
COSTUME SUGGESTIONS: Scruffy clothes, a beard.
SECTIONS: The Giant's Return.

Snow, Frost, North Wind and Hail
The four weather elements are the real baddies of the show. They should be able to sing and move well as a group and on their own. The person playing the Hail should be able to perform simple tap steps or use an umbrella to tap on the stage.
COSTUMES SUGGESTIONS Flamboyant and extrovert to suit each character.
SECTIONS: Winter, The Corner of the Garden, The End?, Encore.

The Child
This part should be played by a small boy (or a girl playing a boy). He should be a strong actor and sweet singer, and should be of fragile appearance.
COSTUME SUGGESTIONS: Tattered clothes and visually different from the other children.
SECTIONS: Awakenings, The End?, Encore.

PROPERTIES

Basic properties are suggested throughout the script. However, these can be as simple or elaborate as resources allow

SET

There are four areas of the stage where action takes place. Here are a few suggestions for scenery and furniture.

(a) The Garden. The main part of the stage.
At least two trees are set upstage left and upstage right. These trees could be mounted on wooden blocks large enough for a child or two to stand on or they could be simply represented by step-ladders as were used in one production. Each tree could rotate and be painted or dressed on one side to depict the tree in winter and on the reverse to depict the tree in spring. The trees are turned at different times during the show to indicate the alternating seasons. The different seasons could also be achieved through the use of lighting.

(b) The Gardeners' Bench. Downstage right

An ordinary garden bench or other garden furniture is set downstage right. This is where the four Gardeners are based. They can narrate from here or elsewhere on the stage, but they should return to the bench when they are observing the action.

(c) The Giant's Castle. Downstage left

A large chair set downstage left represents a room inside the Giant's castle. More elaborate scenery could be used to depict this.

(d) The Giant's Wall

The wall could be as simple or elaborate as resources allow. Possible suggestions are: (1) a piece of hardboard on wheels or castors painted to look like a wall, (2) a piece of painted material held taut by members of the company or (3) children in a line with brick designs on their T-shirts. The wall is not visible at the start of the show —it is set during Section 4 and then struck during Section 10. If possible the wall should be moved on and off stage at these two points. If this is not possible then it should be permanently set upstage centre between the trees and covered up when not in use.

LIGHTING

Great effects and atmosphere can be achieved through lighting and if used thoughtfully will reduce the need for elaborate scenery. The ability to isolate individual areas of the stage with the creative use of specials, stage washes and follow-spots will add a great deal to the performance and the audience's enjoyment.

MUSIC NOTES

The show is divided into fourteen sections of music and each section should segue from one to the next as seamlessly as possible.

There are two versions of Section 4 (Build a Wall). The first is the longer version which includes historical facts and figures about Hadrian's Wall and the Great Wall of China. The second version is greatly simplified and can be used if there are time and technical restraints.

Metronome markings have been printed in the score. In order to recreate the appropriate mood for each section it is essential that these are adhered to as closely as possible.

A demonstration CD containing all of the music in the show can be hired from Samuel French Ltd. This recording must be used for perusal and learning purposes only.

The show can be performed with a live accompaniment or with the use of a backing CD (see below).

LIVE ACCOMPANIMENT

The piano score printed in this book can be used for rehearsal purposes and performance accompaniment.

The piano forms the core of the orchestration and therefore the show can be performed quite effectively with piano alone. To add interest to the musical accompaniment, other instruments can be added:

2nd Keyboard
Bass Guitar
Reed I (Flute, Clarinet, Alto Sax)
Brass I (Trumpet, Flugelhorn)
Bass Guitar
Percussion (Drum Kit, Glockenspiel, Bell Tree, Triangle, etc.)

Band parts are available for hire from Samuel French Ltd.

RECORDED BACKING

A CD of the backing track for use during the performance is available on hire from Samuel French Ltd.

VOCAL OPTIONS

There is very little use of harmony in the show. When the vocal line does divide, smaller notes have been printed as the optional harmony line. These notes can be omitted if required.

David Perkins

Other titles with music by David Perkins
and book and lyrics by Jenifer Toksvig,
published by Samuel French Ltd:

The Curious Quest for the Sandman's Sand
Skool & Crossbones
Shake, Ripple & Roll
Pandemonium! (a Greek Myth-adventure)

The authors' website at www.toksvig-perkins.com has photographs of the original productions, soundbites and other useful information.

ACKNOWLEDGEMENTS

The authors would like to thank
the following people for their continuing support:

Julia Burgess
James Barber and the Yvonne Arnaud Theatre, Guildford
The YAT Youth Theatre Kids (and their parents!)
John Harris
Jenifer Toksvig

... and not forgetting

Oscar Wilde

*Dedicated to everyone
involved with the 1995, 1999
and 2002 productions of*
The Selfish Giant *at Guildford's
Yvonne Arnaud Theatre.*

THE SELFISH GIANT
A children's musical
based on the short story by Oscar Wilde

The stage is divided into four areas. The main area is the Garden, DR is the Gardeners' bench, DL is the Giant's Castle, and the Giant's wall (See Production Notes on page x)

In the garden, there are at least two trees set UL and UR. The trees represent spring. (See Production Notes on page x). There is a large chair DL to represent the Giant's castle. Beside the Giant's chair is a teddy-bear, a winter hat and scarf, a big handkerchief and a walking-stick. Beside the Gardeners' bench is a watering-can, a trug containing four small pieces of fruit, trowels or small garden forks, four sunflowers, a builder's hard hat and various empty flowerpots as dressing

In the orignal production, as the audience arrived, a small boy dressed in contemporary casual clothes sat under one of the trees, reading a book

Overture

Towards the end of the Overture the boy finished reading his book, stood up and exited slowly

Section 1. The Garden

Four Gardeners enter during the first few bars of the music and pick up their trugs. Special lighting comes up on the Gardeners

As the Gardeners begin to sing, the Lights snap to a full spring wash effect

Gardeners (*singing*) There once was a lovely garden with grass that was soft and green.
It was the kind of garden that is very rarely seen,
And here and there all about the ground, such lovely flowers stood around
And made a pleasant scene.

The Flowers enter

Gardeners
Flowers
Oh, what a wonderful place this is!
Oh, what a marvellous place to live!
Oh, what a marvellous, wonderful, marvellous wonder
This garden is!

On the following line, the Gardeners perform a sleight-of-hand trick with their pieces of fruit to make it appear that they are picking fruit from the trees

Gardeners The trees that grew in the garden in the springtime bore rich fruit,
The best plums and pears and peaches, which no one could dispute.
The beauty is hard to describe in words, but it made a stop for migrating birds
Who would sit and sing *en route*.

The Birds enter

Gardeners ⎫
Flowers   ⎬ Oh, what a wonderful place this is!
Birds   ⎭ Oh, what a marvellous place to live!
Oh, what a marvellous, wonderful, marvellous,
Oh, what a wonderful, marvellous, wonderful,
Oh, what a marvellous, wonderful, marvellous wonder
This garden is!

The lighting cross-fades to specials on the Gardeners

Gardener 1 Now, the garden belonged to a Giant who was many miles away.
Gardener 2 He was staying with a friend quite near Land's End,
Gardener 3 And an empty garden ...
Gardener 4 Such a tempting place to play.

Gardeners So, every day when school was done,
The village children one by one
(*Speaking*) Would creep inside and play.

Section 2. How Happy We Are

The Lights cross-fade to a gloomy wash effect

During the first few bars of the music the Children creep in through the audience

The music suddenly represents a false alarm and the Children all jump with fright. One brave child goes ahead to check that the garden is empty and finally gives the all-clear signal with a loud whistle. The rest of the Children rush in and they all start playing in the garden

The Lights snap to a full spring wash effect

Children (*singing*) How happy we are, how happy we are,
The garden's our playground and happy we are.
The Giant's not here, so we play ev'ry day,
We're happy to come here as long as we may.

How lucky we are, how lucky we are,
We're privileged children and lucky we are.
We don't have to worry, the Giant's not here,
We play in this garden, we've nothing to fear.

We play in the autumn with leaves on the ground,
We play in the winter, throw snowballs around,
We play in the summer, eat fruit from the trees
And in springtime pick flowers that dance in the breeze!

The music continues as the Children play

How merry we are, how merry we are,
How long will it last? Will it fade like a star?
Whatever the weather, we've made it our plan,
To stay here forever, as long as we can.

How happy we are, how happy we are,
The garden's our playground and happy we are.
The Giant's not here, so we play ev'ry day,
We're happy to come here as long as we may.

How happy we are!
How happy we are!
How happy we are!
How happy we are!

Section 3. The Giant's Return

The Children freeze in tableau

The Lights slowly cross-fade to specials on the Gardeners

Gardener 1 (*singing*) Meanwhile down in Cornwall,
Gardener 2 A mile from Lizard Bay,
Gardener 3 The Giant, who was visiting his friend the Cornish Ogre,
Gardener 4 Was coming to the end of his stay.

The music continues to underscore

The Giant and the Cornish Ogre enter from opposite sides and meet DC in front of the tableau. The Giant is wearing a hat and coat, and is holding a suitcase

A large pool of light comes up DC

Giant (*speaking*) Well, well, well,
Gardeners Said the Giant.

Giant (*singing*)	I'm afraid that that is that. I've said all that I've got to say, I've nothing more to add.
Gardeners (*speaking*)	The Giant and the Ogre had been talking for seven years, But as the Ogre pointed out,
Cornish Ogre	A rest would suit my ears!
Giant (*singing*)	It's time to leave this dismal place and go back to my garden, My lovely birds, my flowers and my trees. Farewell, my Cornish friend, my visit's at an end, I'll take my leave of absence, if you please. I want to see my lovely garden.

The Cornish Ogre exits

The Lights slowly cross-fade to a gloomy wash effect, with a follow-spot on the Giant

The Giant faces the audience and walks menacingly on the spot. The Gardeners walk amongst the motionless children trying to warn them

Gardener 1	Oh horror, oh horror, the Giant's coming home, You'd better be careful, the Giant's coming home.
Gardener 1 **Gardener 2**	Oh horror, oh horror, the Giant's coming home, You'd better be careful, the Giant's coming home.
Gardener 1 **Gardener 2** **Gardener 3**	Oh horror, oh horror, the Giant's coming home, You'd better be careful, the Giant's coming home.
Gardeners	Oh horror, oh horror, the Giant's coming home, You'd better be careful, the Giant's coming home.

The Giant moves into the garden

The Lights snap to a full spring wash effect

The Children scream and run around in fright

Giant	What are you doing here? What do I see? My garden is crawling with children! My anger is brewing, there's no guarantee That I'll let them go free and not kill them!
Children	Oh horror, oh horror, the Giant's returned, He's back and it looks like he's angry. We'll have to escape! We're greatly concerned! It looks like he could be quite hungry!

The Selfish Giant

Giant
Get out! Get out!
For this garden's my garden, not yours it's mine!
Get out! Get out!
Get out of my beautiful garden!

Children	**Giant**	**Gardeners**
Oh horror, oh horror, the Giant's returned, He's back and it looks like he's angry. We have to escape! We're greatly concerned! It looks like he could be quite hungry!	Get out! Get out! This garden's my garden, not yours it's mine! Get out! Get out! And never return again!	Ah…(etc.)
Oh horror, oh horror, the Giant's returned, He's back and it looks like he's angry. We have to escape! We're greatly concerned! It looks like he could be quite hungry!	Get out! Get out This garden's my garden, not yours it's mine! Get out! Get out! And never return again!	Ah…(etc.)

Giant
For my garden's my garden, not yours it is mine!
And I'll not allow children to play in it.
I'll build a high wall and I'll put up a sign
To describe what I'll do if you stray in it.

I'll build a high wall
And I'll put up a sign.
For my garden's my garden, my own and precious garden,
Now and for ever more!

Get out! Get out! Get out!

The Children are terrified and run out of the garden

Black-out

Section 4. Build a Wall

There are two versions of this song depending on the time available and capabilities of the cast. (See Music Notes on page xii) During the song, the wall is brought on stage or revealed. (See Production Notes on page xi)

A spotlight comes up on the Giant

Version 1 (Longer)

During the chorus, the Giant acts as a building site foreman and supervises the Gardeners as they build a wall around his garden. During the verses, the Gardeners enjoy acting out the historical episodes mentioned

Giant (*singing*) If you want a peaceful, quiet life
Then listen here, take my advice.
If you want to keep your home secure,
Then what I say will reassure.
"What is it?" I hear you cry,
Well …

One of the Gardeners throws the hard hat to the Giant who catches it. The Giant puts it on

It's a spot of DIY.

Menacing lighting effects snap up on the construction area or wall

Build a wall, build a wall,
Make it strong, make it tall,
Build it high, to the sky, to defy.

Giant
Gardeners Build a wall, build a wall,
Make it strong, make it tall,
Build it high, to the sky, to defy.

Gardener 1 Your enemies to keep at bay,
The hist'ry books tell all.
Gardener 2 If you want folks to stay away
Then get yourself a wall.
Gardener 3 In Roman times they did the same,
They knew the latest tricks.
Gardener 4 (*as the Emperor Hadrian*)
The Emp'ror Hadrian made his name
By doing things with bricks.
Gardener 1
Gardener 2 His wall, it stretched for eighty miles and twenty-one feet tall,
Gardener 3 It was the largest on his files
Gardener 4 And kept the peace for all.

Giant (*speaking*) Oy! What do you think you're doing?!

(*Singing*) Build a wall, build a wall,
Make it strong, make it tall,
Build it high, to the sky, to defy.

The Selfish Giant

Giant ⎫ Gardeners ⎭	Build a wall, build a wall, Make it strong, make it tall, Build it high, to the sky, to defy.
Gardener 1 Gardener 4 (*as a Chinese Emperor*)	The Chinese Emp'ror, So they say,
Gardener 1 Gardener 2	Two thousand years ago, Fell out with nomads from the north And told them where to go.
Gardener 3	He called the local builders in To build a massive wall.
Gardener 4 (*as a Chinese Emperor*)	It stopped his troubles, stopped the din And kept things cool for all.
Gardener 1 ⎫ Gardener 2 ⎬ Gardener 3 ⎪ Gardener 4 ⎭	It stretched for eighteen hundred miles And twenty five feet tall, It was the largest on his files And kept things cool for all.

Giant (*speaking*) I don't pay you to stand around doing nothing! Come on ...

(*Singing*)	Build a wall, build a wall, Make it strong, make it tall, Build it high, to the sky, to defy.
Giant ⎫ Gardeners ⎭	Build a wall, build a wall, Make it strong, make it tall, Build it high, to the sky, to defy.
	Build a wall! Build a wall! Build a wall!

On the last "Build a wall!" the Giant reveals a large sign saying "Trespassers Will Be Eaten!". A spotlight comes up on the sign

      Build a wall!

Version 2 (Shorter)

In this shorter version of the song, the wall is built during chorus by the Giant with the help of the Gardeners

Giant If you want a peaceful, quiet life,
Then listen here, take my advice.
If you want to keep your home secure,
Then what I say will reassure.
"What is it?" I hear you cry,
Well …

One of the Gardeners throws the hard hat to the Giant who catches it. The Giant puts it on

It's a spot of DIY.

Menacing lighting effects snap up on the construction area or wall

Build a wall, build a wall,
Make it strong, make it tall,
Build it high, to the sky, to defy.

Giant
Gardeners   Build a wall, build a wall,
Make it strong, make it tall,
Build it high, to the sky, to defy.

Build a wall!
Build a wall!
Build a wall!

On the last "Build a wall!" the Giant reveals a large sign saying "Trespassers Will Be Eaten!" A spotlight comes up on the sign

Build a wall!

Section 5. Outside the Garden

The Children enter in front of the wall

The sign is still in full view and the stage is lit with a gloomy wash effect

Special lighting comes up on the Gardeners

Gardener 1
Gardener 2   The poor children had nowhere to play.
They attempted to play on the road, but the road it was dusty,
And full of hard stones.

A child trips over

Gardener 3
Gardener 4   They only could wander around,
They'd wander around the high wall when their lessons
   were over,
And talk of old times.

The Selfish Giant

Child 1 Do you remember the beautiful garden?
The flowers, the birds and the trees?
The fragrance that drifted in springtime
From the blossom that fell in the breeze.

Child 1
Child 2 With grass soft and gentle beneath us,
We never got injured or hurt,
And the memories we cherish won't leave us
For we now have to play in the dirt.

Children Oh, what a day that was,
Oh, what a day that was,
Oh, what a day, a glorious day!
Oh, what a day that was.

Child 1 The Giant has really upset us,
He's selfish, he's cruel and he's bad.
We've lost all the good things for ever
For he's taken the best thing we had.

Child 2 If only the Giant would share it,
There's plenty of room for us all.
If only he'd take down that notice,
If only he'd knock down that wall.

Children Oh, what a day that was,
Oh, what a day that was,
Oh, what a day, a glorious day!
Oh, what a day that was.

During the final bars of music the Children exit slowly

The Lights slowly fade to Black-out

The two trees set UL and UR are turned around so that they represent winter. The wall is moved UC and set behind the trees

Special lighting comes up on the Gardeners and a gloomy wash effect comes up on the garden

Section 6. Inside the Garden

The Gardeners hold sunflowers. The Giant wanders sadly around his garden dressed in his woolly hat, coat and scarf

Gardener 1 (*singing*) Then came the spring and with it great joy.
Gardener 2 There were flowers and birds for the world to enjoy.
Gardeners But it was still winter (*they put their sunflowers down by their sides*) in the selfish Giant's garden.
His thoughtless behaviour Mother Nature could not pardon.

Gardener 1	The trees would not blossom.
Gardener 2	The birds would not sing.
Gardener 3	Once, a flower appeared,
Gardener 4	As she thought it was spring.

A follow-spot comes up

A Flower enters and performs a short dance

The Giant watches from behind a tree

At the end of the dance, the Flower notices the threatening sign

Flower (*speaking*) "Trespassers Will be Eaten", what a horrible sign,
The children have left here and so shall I.

The Flower exits

The Giant follows the Flower willing her not to leave. He fails and walks to his chair, slowly and sadly

The Lights return to the gloomy winter effect, with special lighting on the four Gardeners. Dry-ice or smoke effects begin

Section 7. Winter

Gardener 1 (*speaking*) The only people who were pleased were the Snow …

Snow enters

Snow All right?!
Gardener 1 And the Frost.

Frost enters

Frost Hello!

Frost and Snow dance. As they dance they laugh crazily

Snow ⎱	(*singing*)	We're cold, we're bad and we're wet.
Frost ⎰		We're two you'll never forget.
Snow		I'm the Snow and I cover the ground
		With my great white coat which I swirl around!
Snow ⎱		We're cold, we're bad and we're wet.
Frost ⎰		We're two you'll never forget.
Frost		I'm the Frost and I cause complaint
		'Cause, I freeze the world with my can of paint!

The Selfish Giant

Snow ⎱
Frost ⎰ We're cold and we're nasty, so horribly nasty
And terribly nice we ain't!

Snow (*speaking*) Spring has forgotten this garden...
Frost (*speaking*) So we will live here all the year round!

They dance and continue to laugh hysterically

Gardener 2 (*speaking*) And they invited the North Wind to pay a visit.

Snow ⎱
Frost ⎰ (*shouting*) Oy! Wind!

North Wind enters

Wind (*singing*) I'm the Wind from the North.
I whistle, I blow and I roar!
I'm wrapped in furs to keep me warm
And wherever I go I cause a storm.
I blow and I whistle, I sting like a thistle,
I'm wicked, it's quite the norm.

North Wind dances a wild, swirly dance. He collapses exhausted in the arms of Snow and Frost

(*Speaking*) This is a delightful spot, we must ask the Hail to pay a visit.

Snow ⎱
Frost ⎱ (*shouting*) Hail!
Wind ⎰

Hail enters. He dances a short dance, preferably tap or by tapping his umbrella on the ground. He continues on tapping as he sings

Hail I like to rattle around, (*tap-tap*)
My hailstones flatten the ground. (*Tap-tap*)
I crush, I squash, I bend, I break,
My tapping gives your head an ache.
I rattle, I prattle, I tittle, I tattle,
A mis'rable life to make! (*Tap-tap*)

Snow ⎱
Frost ⎱ For we'll serve up a nasty dish,
Wind ⎰ 'Cause we're in league with Michael Fish!
Hail ⎰

Snow ⎱ We're cold and we're nasty, so horribly nasty,
Frost ⎰
Wind I blow and I whistle, I sting like a thistle,
Hail I rattle, I prattle, I tittle, I tattle

Snow
Frost   A mis'rable life to make.
Wind   To make!
Hail

They remain frozen in tableau during the following

Black-out

Special lighting comes up on the Giant DL

Section 8. The Giant Laments

The Giant sits in his chair looking out miserably at the wintry scene below. He has a bad cold and is huddled in his coat, winter hat and scarf, holding a hanky to his nose. He tries to seek comfort in his last remaining friend, his teddy bear!

Giant (*singing*) I cannot understand why the spring is late in coming,
I hope the weather changes soon.
This bitter winter weather is nothing short of numbing,
I hope the weather changes soon.
And flowers in my garden bloom,
And birds show off their springtime plume,
And sunshine will replace the gloom,
And defrost my frozen plumbing,
My frozen plumbing!

The Giant gives an almighty sneeze and blows his nose loudly

A gloomy winter lighting effect comes up, with special lighting on the four Gardeners

Gardeners But the spring never came and neither did the summer,
So it was always winter there.
And all day he'd complain 'cause he couldn't get a plumber,
"Life", he said, "is so unfair."

Gardener 1 (*speaking*) And the Snow!

Snow does a little dance

Gardener 2 (*speaking*) And the Frost!

Frost does a little dance

Gardener 3 (*speaking*) And the Wind!

Wind does a little dance

Gardener 4 (*speaking*) And the Hail!

Hail does a little dance

Gardeners (*speaking*) Danced about through the trees.

Snow, Frost, Wind and Hail dance through the trees and exit

Black-out. Dry-ice or smoke effects finish

The two trees UL and UR are turned so that they now represent spring

Special lighting comes up on the Gardeners and the Giant

Section 9. Awakenings

Gardener 2 One morning the Giant was lying awake in bed when he heard some lovely music.

Giant (*singing*)	How sweet to my ears this music is, What beautiful sounds, what joy it brings. It must be the King's musicians passing by.
Gardeners	So out of his bed the Giant climbed, And walked to the window and looked outside, And a most delightful sight met his sleepy eyes.

Spring wash lighting effect slowly comes up on the garden

The Birds enter and fly around the trees

Giant (*speaking*) It's the birds, it's only the birds singing! This is the most beautiful music in the world!

Gardener 3 And through a little hole in the wall, the children crept in.

The Children enter. A child or two sits or stands at the base of the trees

Gardener 4 And some sat in the branches of the trees.
Gardener 1 Spring had returned to the Giant's garden.

The Flowers enter

Children (*singing*) Spring has returned to the Giant's garden.
Is it confirmed? Is the Giant really dead?
All depends on your point of view,
Just a rumour or could be true.
We are taking a chance, it must be said.

Winter has gone and has left this place alone.
Birds sing their song and the grass is soft and green.
All the flowers are standing proud,
The sky is blue and without a cloud,
And the Giant's nowhere to be seen.

All the joys of spring are with us,
Happiness and joy to give us.
Ev'ry day we'll come and play, and once again have fun!
No more giants, no more baddies,
Mums won't worry, nor will daddies.
We'll be safe and free from danger,
Each and ev'ryone.

Giant   Children in my garden, what a pretty sight!
Do they think I've gone away or vanished in the night?
All depends on your point of view,
Just a vision or could be true,
Perhaps it might be time to reunite.

Children ⎫
Gardeners ⎬ All the joys of spring are with us,
Flowers   ⎪ Happiness and joy to give us.
Birds   ⎭
Ev'ry day we'll come and play, and once again have fun!
No more giants, no more baddies,
Mums won't worry, nor will daddies.
We'll be safe and free from danger,
Each and ev'ryone.

The Gardeners sing the La's in harmony

La La La La La La La La
La La La La La La La La
We'll be safe and free from danger,
Each and ev'ry one.
Each and ev'ry one.
Yeah!

The Child enters R and turns the UR tree back to represent winter. He stands underneath the tree, looking up into it

The lighting slowly cross-fades to a special winter effect on the tree UR and specials on the Gardeners and Giant

The Children freeze in tableau away from the Child

Section 10. The Corner of the Garden

Gardener 1 It was a lovely scene, only in one corner it was still winter …
Gardener 2 It was the furthest corner of the garden and in it was standing a little boy.
Gardener 3 The tree was covered in frost and snow and the boy couldn't reach the branches as he was too tiny.
Gardener 4 The Giant looked at the little boy and his heart melted.

The Child tries to reach the branches of the tree and the Giant watches

Giant (*singing*)	How selfish I have been,
	Now I know why the spring did not come here.
	How selfish I have been.
	How selfish I have been.
	I will put that little child in the top of the tree,
	I will knock down the wall and my garden will be free
	For the children to play in for ever more.
	How selfish I have been.

Gardener 1 (*speaking*) So he crept downstairs, opened the front door softly and went out into the garden.

The Giant moves into the garden

The Lights snap to a spring wash effect on the garden

The Children are terrified

Children (*singing*)	Oh horror, oh horror, the Giant's not dead,
	He's alive and it looks like he's angry.
	We'll have to escape!
	We're greatly concerned!
	It looks like he could be quite hungry!

The Children exit

Giant	Come back! Come back!
	For the garden's your garden, it's yours not mine!
	Come back! Come back!
	Come back to your beautiful garden!

Gardeners (*speaking*) And Winter returned to the garden.

The Lights fade to the winter effect. A special light comes up on the UR tree. Dry-ice or smoke effects begin

Snow, Frost, Wind and Hail enter and turn the UL tree back to represent winter

Gardener 3 Only the little boy did not run, for his eyes were so full of tears that he did not see the Giant coming.

Gardener 4 And the Giant walked up behind him, took him gently by the hand and put him up into the tree.

The Giant walks over to the Child and lifts him into the tree. The Child is so happy that he hugs the Giant

Snow, Frost, Wind and Hail exit and the Children run back in

The Children befriend the Giant and he is happy to see them. The two trees are turned back so that they represent spring

The Lights snap to a full spring wash effect. Dry-ice or smoke effects finish

Giant It's your garden, now, little children.
Gardener 1 There was only one thing left for the Giant to do...

Giant (*singing*) The hist'ry books ain't always right,
To keep the peace you don't have to fight.
You shouldn't have to build a wall,
It didn't solve things after all.

The Romans and those Chinese folk
Built those walls it was no joke.
But the Germans from the East and West
Took theirs down and did what's best.

And now I'll do the same to mine,
I'll break the wall and take away the sign.

From off stage somebody holds out an axe, so that only their hand and the axe can be seen by the audience

The Giant grabs the axe

The person's hand retreats back off stage

Break the wall, break the wall,
Make it crumble, make it fall.
Smash it down, crash it down
To the ground.

All Break the wall, break the wall,
Make it crumble, make it fall.
Smash it down, crash it down
To the ground.

The Giant smashes the wall with his axe and there is the sound effect of wall crashing down

The wall is destroyed, removed from the stage or concealed and the Children cheer

The Selfish Giant

Section 11. Harmony

During the following the Child exits unseen

Children (*singing*)   Playing in the garden, staying in the garden
Through the seasons of the year.
The Giant has repented, no more discontented,
Now we've nothing more to fear.
He lets us spend the hours, running through the flowers,
Lifts us up into the trees.
Laughing, smiling with us, lovely things to give us,
Doing ev'rything to please.

The Giant is a thoughtful man,
Those selfish days have gone, it's very plain.
His garden is our playground now,
Each day we'll come and play and never run away again.

Children
Gardeners   Playing in the garden, staying in the garden
Through the seasons of the year.
The Giant has repented, no more discontented,
Now we've nothing more to fear.

Giant   How could I have been so bad?
Those selfish days have gone, I swear to you.
This garden is your playground now,
I promise you that what I say is true.

Children	**Giant**	**Gardeners**
Playing in the garden, staying in the garden		Ah … (etc.)
Through the seasons of the year.	How could I have been so bad?	
The Giant has repented, no more discontented,		
Now we've nothing more to fear.	How selfish I have been.	
Playing in the garden, staying in the garden		Ah … (etc.)
Through the seasons of the year.	How could I have been so bad?	
The Giant has repented, no more discontented,		
Now we've nothing more to fear.	How selfish I have been.	
Now we've nothing more to fear.	You've nothing more to fear.	

Giant (*shouting*) Wait!

A slow cross-fade to special lighting on the Giant and UR tree

(*Singing*)	Where is the little boy that I put into the tree?
	Have you seen the little boy, the one that smiled at me?
	The tree it stands quite empty, the tree it stands quite empty,
	The child I cannot see.

The Lights slowly cross-fade to full stage lighting

	Do you know him?
	Have you seen him?
	Do you know where he lives?
	Did you see where he was going?
	Do you know where he is?
	Did you like and did you see how much happiness he gives?
Children	We don't know the little boy, the one that's gone away.
Giant	Be sure to tell him clearly he must come again some day.
Children	But we don't know where he lives and we've not seen him before.
	He isn't even one of us; he looked so very frail and hungry, Tattered clothes and poor.
Giant	Do you know him?
	Have you seen him?
	Do you know where he lives?
Children	We don't know where he lives.
Giant	Did you see where he was going?
	Do you know where he is?
Children	We cannot tell you.
Giant	Did you like and did you see how much happiness he gives?
Children	We do not know
Giant	Do you know him?
	Have you seen him?
	Do you know where he lives?
Children	We don't know where he lives.
Giant	Did you see where he was going?
	Do you know where he is?
Children	We cannot tell you.
Giant	Did you like and did you see how much happiness he gives?
Children	We do not know.

At the end of the song the Giant and the Children freeze in tableau

The Lights slowly fade to Black-out

Section 12. The Passage of Time

Special lighting comes up on the Gardeners

Gardener 1 So every afternoon when school was over, the children came and played with the Giant.

The Children and the Giant come out of tableau and start playing in the garden

The Lights snap to a full spring wash effect on the Children

Gardener 2 But the little child whom the Giant loved was nowhere to be seen.

Giant (*singing*) How I would like to see him again.
　　　　　　　　　How I would like to see him again.
　　　　　　　　　Before I complete my three score and ten,
　　　　　　　　　I'd like to see him again.

Gardener 3 (*speaking*) Years went by and the Giant grew old and feeble. He could not play any more …

The Giant's chair is moved c and he is given his walking-stick. He sits down

The spring wash effect fades slightly. Special lighting comes up on the Gardeners

Gardener 4 So he sat in a huge armchair and watched the children at their games.

Special lighting comes up on the Giant

Giant (*singing*) I'm getting old, alas,
　　　　　　　　　And countless generations pass.
　　　　　　　　　I'm getting old alas.
　　　　　　　　　The years have slipped away
　　　　　　　　　I spend my autumn years shedding happy tears
　　　　　　　　　And watching, just watching the children at their play.

The Children exit

The Giant waves them goodbye

(*Speaking*) I have many beautiful flowers, but the children are the most beautiful flowers of all.

The Lights slowly cross-fade to specials on the Gardeners and a winter wash effect on the garden. Dry-ice or smoke effects begin

Section 13. The End?

Gardener 1 One morning the Giant was sitting in his garden when winter returned.

The Snow, Frost, Wind and Hail enter and turn the tree UL back to winter

Snow ⎫
Frost ⎬ (*singing*) We're cold, we're bad and we're wet.
Wind ⎪   We're four you'll never forget!
Hail ⎭

Giant I do not fear the winter now,
I have no cause to weep.
For flowers that in springtime bloom
Are merely fast asleep!

The Snow, Frost, Wind and Hail exit dejectedly

The Child enters and sits under the tree UR, that is still in spring

Gardener 1 (*speaking*) However, in one corner it was still spring.

Special spring lighting comes up on tree UR. Dry-ice or smoke effects finish

Gardener 2 (*speaking*) It was the furthest corner of the garden and in it was sitting the little boy whom the Giant had loved.

Giant (*singing*) Do I believe my eyes?
It's that little child again, how I've missed him.
Do I believe my eyes?
He mustn't go away.
If he does, I doubt I'll live to see the day
When the child returns again to play
And bless my weary eyes.

Gardener 3 And the Giant got out of his chair ...
Gardener 4 And walked over to the child to meet him.

The Giant walks over to the Child and sees that he has small wounds on his hands and feet

Giant (*singing*) But you are wounded!
Your tiny hands and feet, but they are bleeding!
Who has dared to harm you?
Tell me, so I can take my sword and kill him!

Child But these are the wounds of love.
Giant (*speaking*) Who are you?

The Selfish Giant

Child (*singing*)	Don't you know me?
	Can't you see me?
	Don't you know where I live?
Giant	I don't know where you live.
Child	Do you know where we are going?
	Do you know where that is?
Giant	I cannot tell you.
Child	Only then you'll truly see
	How much happiness I give.
	Once you let me play in your garden.
	Today you shall come with me to my garden.
	My garden which is paradise.

The Lights cross-fade to a heavenly glow

The Child takes the Giant by the hand. The Giant puts down his walking-stick and is slowly led away by the Child upstage between the trees. They exit. As they exit, the Children and the Gardeners enter and line the route

The Children and Gardeners sing on an "ah"

Special lighting comes up on the Gardeners

Gardener 1 (*speaking*) And although the Giant was never seen again, his memory lived on ...
Gardener 2 And all the trees in his beautiful garden blossomed year after year.
Gardener 3 For many generations to follow, children would come and play there.
Gardener 4 And the Giant would always be there with them — in their minds and in their hearts.

The Lights fade to a gentle full stage wash effect

Section 14. Anthem

During the introduction to the song the company move to c. They remain very still during the song

The song is divided vocally into three Groups A to C, with optional harmonies for Groups B and C. If unison singing is preferred, Groups B and C still join in where indicated

One Voice (*singing, from Group A*)
    A love that will never die,
    A light that will always shine,
    A star that will twinkle in the sky
    Until the end of time.

Two Voices (*from Group A*)
As night time becomes the day
And winter becomes the spring,
Sunshine will always follow rain,
To help us smile, to ease the pain.
Joy will blossom within our hearts
And all the birds will sing.

Few Voices (*from Group A*)
The start of a brand new day,
A seed that becomes a tree,
A stream that is dancing on its way
And heading for the sea.

Few more voices (*Groups A and B*)
The gold at a rainbow's end,
The hope that a prayer can bring,
The faith that tomorrow there will be
A better world for all to see.
Joy will blossom within our hearts
And all the birds will sing.

All (*Groups A, B and C*)
Hearts that are mean and cold as ice
And hearts that are hard as stone,
Can melt with a love that's deep inside
And break when the truth is known.

A love that will never die,
A light that will always shine,
A star that will twinkle in the sky
Until the end of time.

The gold at a rainbow's end,
The hope that a prayer can bring,
The faith that tomorrow there will be
A better world for all to see.
Joy will blossom within our hearts
And all the birds will sing.

One Voice Joy will blossom within our hearts
And all the birds will sing.

The Company slowly exits during the final bars of music. One child picks up the Giant's walking-stick, places it under the tree UL *and then exits along with the others*

As they leave, the Lights fade to a special on the tree UL *and then to a Black-out*

Section 14a. Bows

Full spring lighting effect

The Company enter for the Curtain call. After the Giant and the Child have taken their bow they move so that they are detached from the rest of the company for the Encore

Section 14b. Encore

All (*singing*)
Spring has returned to the Giant's garden.
Is it confirmed? Is the Giant really dead?
All depends on your point of view,
Just a rumour or could be true.
We are taking a chance, it must be said.

Winter has gone and has left this place alone.
Birds sing their song and the grass is soft and green.
All the flowers are standing proud,
The sky is blue and without a cloud,
And the Giant's nowhere to be seen.

All the joys of spring are with us,
Happiness and joy to give us.
Ev'ry day we'll come and play, and once again have fun.
No more giants, no more baddies,
Mums won't worry, nor will daddies.
We'll be safe and free from danger,
Each and ev'ryone.

Giant
Child
Children in our garden, what a pretty sight!
Do they think we've gone away or vanished in the night?
All depends on your point of view,
Just a vision or could be true,
Perhaps it might be time to reunite.

All
All the joys of spring are with us,
Happiness and joy to give us.
Ev'ry day we'll come and play, and once again have fun.
No more giants, no more baddies,
Mums won't worry, nor will daddies.
We'll be safe and free from danger,
Each and ev'ryone.

The Gardeners sing the La's in harmony

La La La La La La La La
La La La La La La La La
We'll be safe and free from danger,
Each and ev'ry one!
Each and ev'ry one!
Yeah!

The Lights slowly fade to preset

Section 14c Exit Music (1)

Section 14d Exit Music (2)

FURNITURE AND PROPERTY LIST

Further dressing may be added at the director's discretion.

On stage: Two trees representing spring on one side and winter on the other
Large chair. *Beside the chair*: teddy-bear, winter hat and scarf, big handkerchief, walking-stick
Gardeners' bench. *Beside the bench*: watering-can, trug containing four small pieces of fruit, trowels or small garden forks, four sunflowers, a builder's hard hat, flowerpots
Wall. *On it*:sign saying "Tresspassers Will Be Eaten" (*Or off stage if required see page ix*)
(*If required*) Book for the small boy at the very start of the play

Off stage: Suitcase (**Giant**)
Axe (**Stage-mangement**)

LIGHTING PLOT

The following lighting plot is based on the original production. If resources do not allow such a plot, a simpler one consisting of two or three states could still be very effective.

* Alternative cues if using **Section 4. Build a Wall** (Version 2)

To open: As the audience arrives house lights at full and stage lights at preset

Cue 1	To begin the play *Slow fade house lights and cut preset stage lights*	(Page 1)
Cue 2	The four **Gardeners** enter *Bring up specials on* **Gardeners**	(Page 1)
Cue 3	At the start of the lyric of the song/ at the change of music bar 11 *Snap to full spring stage wash*	(Page 1)
Cue 4	**Gardeners/Flowers/Birds**: " This garden is!" *Cross-fade to specials on* **Gardeners**	(Page 2)
Cue 5	The end of **Section 1. The Garden** *Cross-fade to gloomy stage wash*	(Page 2)
Cue 6	The **Children** start to play in the garden *Snap to full spring stage wash*	(Page 2)
Cue 7	To begin music **Section 3. The Giant's Return** *Slowly cross-fade to special on Gardeners*	(Page 3)
Cue 8	The **Giant** and the **Cornish Ogre** enter *Bring up large pool of light* DC	(Page 3)
Cue 9	The **Cornish Ogre** exits *Slow cross-fade to gloomy stage wash, with a follow-spot on* **Giant**	(Page 4)
Cue 10	The **Giant** moves into the garden *Snap to full spring stage wash*	(Page 4)
Cue 11	The **Children** run out of the garden and exit *Black-out*	(Page 5)
Cue 12	To start music **Section 4. Build a Wall (Versions 1 and 2)** *Bring up spotlight on* **Giant**	(Page 5)

Cue 13	**Giant:** (*singing*) It's a spot of DIY. *Snap to menacing lighting effects on the construction area or wall*	(Page 6)
Cue 14	The **Giant** reveals a large sign saying "Trespassers Will Be Eaten!" *Bring up spotlight on sign*	(Page 7)
*Cue 13	**Giant:** (*singing*) "It's a spot of DIY." *Snap to menacing lighting effects on the construction area or wall*	(Page 8)
*Cue 14	The **Giant** reveals a large sign saying "Trespassers Will Be Eaten!" *Bring up spotlight on sign*	(Page 8)
Cue 15	To start music **Section 5. Outside the Garden** *Bring up specials on the **Gardeners**. Gloomy wash effect on wall and spotlight remaining on sign*	(Page 8)
Cue 16	The **Children** exit slowly *Slow fade to black-out*	(Page 9)
Cue 17	The wall is moved UC and set behind trees; when ready *Bring up specials on **Gardeners** and gloomy stage wash on garden*	(Page 9)
Cue 18	**Gardener 4:** " ... it was spring." *Bring up follow-spot on flower*	(Page 10)
Cue 19	The **Giant** walks to his chair slowly and sadly *Cut follow-spot; revert to previous cue*	(Page 10)
Cue 20	**Snow, Frost, Wind** and **Hail** freeze in tableau *Black-out*	(Page 12)
Cue 21	When ready to start music **Section 8. The Giant Laments** *Bring up special on **Giant** DL*	(Page 12)
Cue 22	The **Giant** sneezes and blows his nose loudly *Bring up gloomy winter wash on garden, with special lighting on gardeners*	(Page 12)
Cue 23	**Snow, Frost, Wind** and **Hail** exit through the trees *Black-out*	(Page 13)
Cue 24	The trees are turned to represent spring, when ready *Bring up special lights on **Gardeners** and **Giant***	(Page 13)
Cue 25	**Gardeners:** (*singing*) "... met his sleepy eyes." *Slow fade up on garden spring wash*	(Page 13)
Cue 26	A **Child** stands underneath tree UR looking up *Slow cross-fade to special winter effect on UR tree, and specials on **Gardeners** and **Giant***	(Page 14)
Cue 27	The **Giant** moves into the garden *Snap to full spring stage wash effect*	(Page 15)

Cue 28	**Gardeners**: " And winter returned to the garden." *Fade to winter stage wash, with special on tree* UR	(Page 15)
Cue 29	The two trees are turned to represent spring *Snap to full spring stage wash effect*	(Page 16)
Cue 30	**Giant**: "Wait!" *Slow cross-fade to special on* **Giant** *and* UR *tree*	(Page 17)
Cue 31	**Giant**: (*singing*) "The child I cannot see." *Slow cross-fade to full stage wash*	(Page 18)
Cue 32	The **Giant** and **Children** freeze in tableau *Slow fade to black-out*	(Page 18)
Cue 33	To start music **Section 12. The Passage of Time** *Bring up specials on* **Gardeners**	(Page 19)
Cue 34	The **Children** and **Giant** come out of tableau and start to play *Snap to full spring stage wash*	(Page 19)
Cue 35	The **Giant** sits down C *Slight fade of full stage wash; special on* **Gardeners**	(Page 19)
Cue 36	**Gardener 4**: " ... children at their games." *Bring up special on* **Giant**	(Page 19)
Cue 37	**Giant**: " ... beautiful flowers of all." *Slow cross-fade to winter wash effect, with specials on* **Gardeners**	(Page 19)
Cue 38	**Gardener 1**: " ... corner it was still spring." *Spring special on tree* UR	(Page 20)
Cue 39	**Child**: (*singing*) " ... which is paradise." *Cross-fade lights to heavenly glow*	(Page 21)
Cue 40	At the end of the **Children/Gardeners** singing on an "ah" *Bring up specials on* **Gardeners**	(Page 21)
Cue 41	**Gardener 4**: " ... their minds and in their hearts." *Fade to gentle full stage wash*	(Page 21)
Cue 42	A child places the walking-stick under the tree L *Slow fade to a special on tree* UL, *then to Black-out*	(Page 22)
Cue 43	To start music **Section 14a. Bows** *Bring up full spring stage wash effect*	(Page 23)
Cue 44	End of music **Section 14b. Encore** after final bow *Slow fade to preset. House lights up*	(Page 24)

EFFECTS PLOT

Cue 1	The **Giant** walks to his chair *Dry-ice or smoke effects*	(Page 10)
Cue 2	**Snow, Frost, Wind** and **Hail** exit through the trees *Cut dry-ice or smoke effect*	(Page 13)
Cue 3	**Gardeners**: " And Winter returned to the garden." *Dry-ice or smoke effects*	(Page 15)
Cue 4	The two trees are turned back so that they represent spring *Cut dry-ice or smoke effect*	(Page 16)
Cue 5	The **Giant** smashes the wall with his axe *Sound of wall crashing down*	(Page 16)
Cue 6	**Giant:** " ... beautiful flowers of all." *Dry-ice or smoke effects*	(Page 19)
Cue 7	**Gardener**: " ... in one corner it was still spring." *Cut dry-ice or smoke effects*	(Page 20)

www.ingramcontent.com/pod-product-compliance
Lightning Source LLC
Chambersburg PA
CBHW061517040426
42450CB00008B/1663